It was a riotous year that witnessed qu
glue-ons, demonstrations, marches and
government worked diligently to prote
every single one of them.

Here it is, the ins and outs, the ups and downs, the cheese and wine.

January

Oh joy, a brand new year. Sadly it looked, felt and smelled distinctly like the old one.

It started with a fireworks and drones display made for TV which was enjoyed by everyone except members of the Cult of the Red Faces who fulminated over it for about two weeks because some of the fireworks were blue and yellow, the colours of the EU flag. You could hear their wailing through concrete.

Their sensitivity bookended the year, as twelve months later, Brexit had gone so well that the government banned civil servants from ever mentioning it by name again.

In the meantime, in America a man dressed like Davy Crockett lead the charge to take over that country on behalf of the ding-a-ling community. The attempt failed because human Ken Doll Mike Pence called Dan Quayle to ask if it would be OK to stage a coup and install Donald Trump as unelected leader. Dan Quayle said "Noe" (old Dan Quayle related "potatoe" spelling joke that you young-uns may have to look up).

Joe Biden, the actual not fake news winner took over as President of the Disunited States of America. His tenure was immediately denounced as a failure by the Republican Party.

Donald Trump consoled himself that he still had Twitter to keep his profile high and his faithful on-side, just before Twitter announced his permanent expulsion.

In Britain, made great again by getting Brexit done, the Covid death toll passed 100,000. Boris Johnson addressed the nation and took full responsibility to find the person responsible.

In a cunning plan to ingratiate himself with diehard labour supporters, Keir Starmer said 'I agree with Boris' a lot.

February

Boris Johnson played dress-up in a laboratory wearing a white coat which made him look less like a scientist and more like the fryer in a chip shop.

Keir Starmer left no trace as leader of the opposition but did sport suspiciously great hair in a lockdown.

A memo went round Tory HQ ordering flags with everything.

Wrapping themselves in the Union Jack, the government plotted to take away the freedom to express dissent or disapproval of the regime, while complaining that the left were stifling freedom of speech.

Priti Patel was deployed as the nation's chief professional dinghy spotter, alongside amateur Nigel Farage who had taken it up as a hobby while at a loose end looking for something else to do now that Johnson had got Brexit done.

March

Nigel Farage joined the Cameo video messaging service and offered to wish that special someone in your life a happy birthday for only £63.75.

The Ever Given got stuck in the Suez Canal interrupting the world's supply of cheap Chinese plastic tat and pretty much everything else you could think of.

The month saw the warmest March day since the last warmest March day. This was caused by global warming due to the steam coming out of foamers' ears at the Oprah Winfrey interview with Hazza and Sparkles. Royal hem-sniffers protested that Oprah gave the two an easy ride and did not ask the sort of tough question that they would have objected to being posed to any other of their royal majesties.

In Bristol, a protest over the protest ban was banned. It was called the Kill the Bill demo, which tabloids deliberately misconstrued to mean the crowd was intent on killing the Old Bill, rather than cancelling the new bill about curtailing rights.

In Clapham, a vigil against Met Police violence was broken up violently by the Met Police.

In politics it was flags with everything. Ministers were, from this moment never seen without at least two flags in the background which jostled for space with portraits of the Queen. This was to demonstrate that, despite their every action being against the interest of the nation, they were definitely patriotic.

Appearing to be patriotic obviated the need to actually be patriotic.

In sensitive snowflake news, the National Trust was attacked for the 'woke re-writing of history' for telling the truth about the money behind many of its buildings. Apparently, denying our history is the only way to honour our history.

To the surprise of no-one, serial love cheat Boris Johnson was outed as the clandestine lover of Jennifer Arcuri by Jennifer Arcuri who joked that she was his "personal penetration tester" in intimate texts that the British people wished had remained secret.

Johnson had texted Arcuri that photos sent by her were "enough to make a bishop kick a hole in a stained glass window", which was enough to make whoever saw the reports of it want to stick barbecue skewers in their eyes.

To take our mind of this, and his other various failings, the Prime Minister dived into his dressing up box again, this time emerging as a B&Q employee. He gawped at pot plants while his personal, tax payer funded photographers searched for his good side.

Not to be outdone, Nigel Farage sent out a creepy video of himself hiding in a tree, offering to send messages to strangers for money.

Keir Starmer went unnoticed for a whole month, as part of his cunning scheme to win the public over to the Labour Party by remaining invisible.

In the comedy world of international art, a cryptocurrency "pioneer" bought an artwork that doesn't exist outside a computer chip. The piece was titled Everydays: The First 5000 Days. It was a jpeg collage of all the pictures that someone who called himself Beeple had drawn and posted online, one each day, since 2007.

It looked like the visual representation of a daily brain fart. We were told it was worth its selling price of $69m because there was only one "official" copy, which made as much sense as anything else that happened this year.

April

Vlad the Insaner was voted Russia's sexiest man by Russians who feared they might not make it to their next birthday if they didn't. And after all, Brad Pitt was named after a hole in the ground, so what chance did he have against His Imperial Hotness?

Prince Harry flipped his baseball cap backwards to walk a dog on a beach, a fashion faux pas for anyone over the age of 16, which the press blamed on Meghan Markle.

An in-depth, no stone unturned government appointed inquiry on racism concluded that there isn't any.

To differentiate his offering from the Tories, Keir Starmer positioned Labour as the party of Law and Order.

In another wizard scheme, Starmer said he would field voters questions during summer in a copy of the Cameron Direct tour of 2008 because David Cameron was just the figure to emulate in order to appeal to Labour's traditional supporters.

Prince Philip died and every TV station provided round the clock coverage, except Channel 4 which won the ratings with Gogglebox.

Newspapers found some unsubtle ways to blame The Duke's death on Meghan, what with all the trouble she'd caused.

In America, a gender reveal party in New Hampshire announced it's a boy with 80lb of explosives that caused an earthquake and damaged buildings across two states. Those parents were passing on those genes!

The stink of corruption swirling around the government got stronger as Johnson started an inquiry, not into the corruption of his regime, but into how we found out about that corruption.

In Covid news, Las Vegas announced topless bars may reopen but dancers must wear face masks. What would the customers look at?

A Japanese man who dated 35 women told each of them he had different birthdays so that he regularly got presents and was arrested for ~~genius~~ fraud.

Boris Johnson's current girlfriend's expensive taste in home decoration, and who paid for the Number 11 flat to resemble a Maharaja's knocking shop, continued to grip the nation, despite the PM telling the public that the public is not interested in that, like he was trying out a Jedi mind trick. Unfortunately for him, he's less a Jedi, more Jabba the Gut.

The world of football was rocked by the realisation that the foreign owners of our biggest clubs were less interested in football than what money they could make out of it. They were sent back to the drawing board after the short-lived prospect of a European Super League was squashed by fans. Boris Johnson took all the credit.

May

On the first of the month, a story appeared which would be hard to beat all year, let alone in May: a free roadside library kiosk for the residents of sleepy Cornholme, near sleepy Todmorden to exchange reading material was being filled with pornography. One outraged villager pinned a note to the box which read: "Whoever is placing the copys (sic) of pornographic literature in here, stop! Cornholme is a God fearing Christian village. If this filth is to your liking may we suggest that you move to the cesspit that is Hebden Bridge"!

Hazza and Sparkles continued to dominate the papers with the press furious at him bringing attention to the royal family's private life, the details of which they published on pages 1,2,3,4,5,6,7,8 and 9 every day for a month.

An Indian variant of the Covid virus was identified and Boris Johnson leapt into action to do nothing while 20,000 people from India sauntered in through our airports and spread it about a lot.

Johnson was trying to engineer a trade deal with India at the time, and was desperate to ingratiate himself with them in an attempt to wrestle a good headline about Brexit, which had nothing to do with keeping the border open to travellers from that country, obviously.

Animal Extinction, an offshoot of Xtinction Rebellion staged a blockade of McDonalds distribution centres, insisting the burger chain go vegan by 2025, by which time pigs would be flying and a cow would jump over the moon.

Speaking of space, NASA and Barak Obama hinted that there may in fact be aliens among us. Initial suspicions point to Priti Patel.

Dominic Cummings presented himself to the joint inquiry of the Health and Social Care Committee and Science and Technology Committee which, according to the parliamentary website, "considers what lessons can be drawn from the Government's handling of the pandemic that could be applied now and in the future". The first lesson was that, by his own admission, Dominic Cummings should not have been left in charge and Boris Johnson should not have left in charge and Matt Hancock really, really should not have been left in charge.

Hancock subsequently appeared himself and made clear that nothing was his fault, it was all like that when he got there. If only Matt Hancock had listened to his "gut" and ignored those pesky scientists we would all have been saved. Oh, and he doesn't lie. He was quite insistent on that point.

June

In cricket news, a man got the largest round of applause of the day for managing to put on a bright yellow cagoule after struggling with it in the stands at Lord's while watching England v New Zealand, which tells you everything you need to know about cricket.

Meanwhile, a fisherman from Cape Cod was minding his own affairs, diving to check his lobster pots, when a humpback whale scoped him into its mouth and, after a short while spat him out...or...a humpback whale was minding its own affairs when an awful tasting human entered its mouth without permission.

England started their campaign to win the UEFA European Football Championship, or Euro 2020 as they called it, even though it was cancelled from that year and was taking place in 2021. They began their route to disappointment by being booed by their own fans before they had kicked a ball because they took the knee prior to kick-off. The fans felt the need to boo because they deemed it more necessary to make it all about themselves than to back the national team they were supposed to be supporting.

The G7 meeting took place in the furthest outpost of England, the hard to reach St Ives. The world leaders and their vast retinues had to travel by jet, boat, helicopter and motorcade, creating a carbon footprint that sucked all the oxygen out of Cornwall. Once there, they expressed their determination to save the planet by all means possible, except actually trying.

Prince Charles gave a speech encouraging us to reduce our emissions to stop climate change. He did this with a straight face despite his immediate family living in one manor, two halls, two cottages, three palaces, three lodges, two parks, seven houses and three castles.

In Brexit news, it was going very well, if starting a war over chilled meats is your idea of going very well. The Sausage War, as they were calling it, had broken out. The government said it was surprised that relations were strained between the UK and the EU. Absolutely everything came as a surprise to them including, perhaps, Matt Hancock canoodling with an underling and the CCTV footage from his office appearing in the papers six weeks later.

The lucky woman was also married to someone else and was hired by Hancock after what his aides said was a "vigorous process"!

Then, after Hancock resigned, Bodge said he fired him and declared the matter closed. Nothing to see here, at least nothing he hadn't done many times before.

In an eagerly anticipated development, the USA released its UFO files and concluded that it had no idea what those things are, which was not the revelation we were hoping for.

July

Teenagers were using lemon juice on their Covid home test kits to get a false positive so they could bunk off school, a trick they were sharing on TikTok which the government said was "unhelpful". Teens said "whatevah".

Two men were arrested in India after saying cow urine and dung was not a cure for Covid-19 on social media.

Erendro Leichombam, an activist, and Kishorechandra Wangkhem, a journalist, refuted claims made by the Prime Minister Narendra Modi's party that cow excrement can protect against coronavirus. The men were dragged from their houses in the state of Manipur and arrested after local BJP party members reported their posts to the police. Pictures were published of men covered in cow dung and praying to catch Covid, for their sense of smell to disappear.

In Britain, Boris Johnson announced the country would re-open during a huge spike in cases. What could possibly go wrong?

After coming into contact with Covid sufferer Health Secretary Sajid "Super Saj Man" Javid, the PM was required to self-isolate. Being Bodge, he decided to join a "new scheme" that meant he didn't have to. The tsunami of ire that greeted that decision made him U-turn within three hours and suffer isolation like the rest of us. Except, he was doing it in a palace in thousands of acres of rolling countryside, with hot and cold servants on tap and everything paid for. By us.

A couple of rich dipsticks travel to near-space for ten minutes. Branson is first and the breathless commentary from his personal commentator told us to remember where we were when this day happened. No-one committed this to memory.

Bezos was second. He looked like he was attempting to re-join his alien people by launching himself at them in what looked like a giant sex-toy. On landing back here, he sported a ludicrously huge Stetson hat from under which the world's richest man thanked Amazon customers and workers because "you paid for this". His audience were unsure whether that was interstellar top-grade trolling or he was so disconnected he didn't understand how that message would be received by his minimum-wage staff.

Prince Harry, out of Hazza and Sparkles, announced he had a four book publishing deal. Critics expressed their outrage at their contents before he had written a word.

The Tokyo Olympics started but was hampered by Boris Johnson not taking part in the zip wire event but was greatly enhanced by the skateboarders who seemed like the only people there actually having fun.

An achievement unrelated to sporting excellence gained nearly the most attention of anything at the games: Tom Daley's knitting skills.

August

Brexit was leaving supermarket shelves empty, the threat of inflation hung over us, unemployment looked set to sky-rocket, the virus was infecting thousands a week, the regime seemed to be run by an offshoot of the Mafia, the world was under threat of annihilation from climate change and all anyone could think of was how to stop the government executing Geronimo the llama which had tested positive for bovine TB.

The climate threat was outlined in a report from the UN that said we are at code red for humanity. Governments around the world leapt into action to say that it really is awful and something should be done.

Joe Biden honoured Donald Trump's huge and tremendous deal with the Taliban and pulled US troops out of Afghanistan. We follow, with no discernible plan of action, and the entirely predictable thing, that no-one in government predicted, happened.

Tetchy angular humanoid Dominic "Deckchair" Raab, the Foreign Secretary, didn't get up from his holiday sun-lounger to do anything about protecting our interests and people, claiming that it wouldn't have made any difference. This was a pretty unique excuse even for a current minister: that he is, essentially, useless.

Afghanistan erupted in turmoil, a suicide bomber struck, the people who helped the British troops were left behind to meet their deaths at the hands of the Taliban but the British showed more concern about the plan to get animals from a rescue charity onto a plane out of there.

A public campaign was started to add a penis to the dragon on the Welsh flag, all other problems in Wales having apparently been solved.

September

A good looking young British woman of Romanian/Chinese descent won a tennis match and caused some Britons to make an exception to their "Romanians go home" message. She also caused many to find a previously absent interest in women's tennis.

Bodger Johnson performed a cabinet reshuffle but he was still captain of this Titanic failure, so the direction of travel remained unchanged and iceberg-bound.

Empty shelves in the supermarkets, crops rotting in the fields and a huge lack of lorry drivers were said to threaten Christmas. The shortages of beer in pubs, lack of blood test vials and rising prices all have nothing to do with Brexit, which is going very well, the government assured us.

In other news, David Frost, the megamind who negotiated the deal with the EU said that by upholding their end of the contract, the EU were being mean to us.

Emergency work visas were issued to tempt foreign lorry drivers to come and save Christmas for the people who had been yelling at them to go back to where they came from for the past five years.

Few applied, which we took to be an indication of their lack of British patriotism..

Meanwhile, fights broke out as the nation panicked and queued for petrol after the government advised us not to panic. 80% of England's petrol stations ran out of petrol, queues of hours formed at those which still had stocks and essential workers were stranded at home.

Boris Johnson rummaged in his dressing-up box for something especially amusing to take our minds off it.

October

According to the press, Kate Middleton debuted a "new sleek bouncy look" to her hair, which seemed to be exactly the same as before. By contrast, Meghan Markle was still the Wicked Witch of the West, so nobody cared about her 'do.

David Frost announced that our Brexit deal, which was sold to us as a great deal for Britain, is apparently a terrible deal for Britain that needed to be renegotiated to provide for extra unicorns and more sunlit uplands. The man who negotiated the deal determined to find out which idiot negotiated that deal.

In related Brexit news, farmers started to burn their livestock on pyres just to get rid of them because they couldn't get them processed as there was a lack of EU abattoir workers to turn them into food that could fit in our fridges. It might have smelled like a barbecue, but it wasn't.

The Chancellor, Rishi Sunak delivered a budget. He boasted that spending on things we rely on would be back to where they were in 2010, forgetting which party had been in power since then.

The details of the budget meant bankers were to be taxed less, while everyone else was to be taxed more. Furthermore, in order to "level up", the tax on champagne was reduced and just before the Cop26 climate change conference, the cost of flying within the UK was cut.

Meanwhile, the government forced their party's MPs to vote to allow privately owned water companies to discharge untreated sewage into our rivers.

We had possibly reached Peak Tory.

In travel news, campaigners Insulate Britain continued to stop traffic on the M25 forcing one irate driver to attack them with bagpipe music.

In related news, an eco-protester and carpenter appeared for a grilling on The Mike Graham radio talk show. Under intense questioning, he maintained that wood was a sustainable building material as you can grow it. He kept an admirably straight face while being told by host Mike Graham that concrete is also a sustainable building material, as you can grow that too.

After a tidal wave of on-line ridicule, Graham managed to make it worse by insisting for days that you can, in fact, grow concrete and invited concrete growing experts on air to back him up.

November

The Tory party was suddenly up to its eyeballs in sewage. Not the sewage that it allowed companies to keep pouring into our rivers and off our coasts, but the sewage of sleaze that came at it like a brown tidal wave and broke over the whole lot of them.

One of the most eye-catching incidents was the ex-Attorney General Sir Geoffrey Cox who, while an MP, earned millions of pounds working for people other than the British electorate in places like the British Virgin Islands, while the rest of us were stuck here because of the Covid flight ban restrictions.

While there, he voted on parliamentary business by having an MP here do it for him. There was also the small point that he earned that money, while parliament was sitting and he was supposed to be working for his constituents. And there was the fact that he was actually helping the BVI with legal advice in a case of corruption brought by the actual UK government, of which he was a part. You couldn't make it up.

As with all the other allegations of sleaze, he apparently did no wrong, broke no rules, all allowed, perfectly normal, nothing to see here.

The Prime Minister bravely ran away when the Commons debated the allegations. He ran to a hospital for a photo shoot. Those pictures showed that he was the only person in that place not wearing a mask for the benefit of the patients.

On the subject of MPs taking second, third and fourth jobs, international trade secretary Anne-Marie Trevelyan said she would not back a ban on MPs having second jobs "because it brings a richness to our role as members of parliament." It certainly does, and either that's top grade trolling there, or she really wasn't listening to what she was saying.

In royal news, the tabloids reported that Kate looked ravishing in her recycled green gown and updated hairstyle and that Meghan was still world's worst person.

From a packed list of exceptional, prize winning dopes, the Plank of the Year Award was won by Don Valley's Conservative MP, Nick Fletcher, who, in an outstanding entry, gave a Westminster speech on the subject of International Men's Day and said "In recent years we have seen Doctor Who, the Ghostbusters, Luke Skywalker and the Equalizer all replaced by women, and men are left with the Krays and Tommy Shelby. Is there any wonder we are seeing so many young men committing crime?"

The only non-fictional characters there are the Krays, both of whom have been dead long enough not to affect those mourning Luke Skywalker's non-existent sex change.

Mr Fletcher wins the Plank of the Year Award but maybe it should be jointly held with the people of Don Valley who voted him in?

December

Last Christmas, when we were all being good boys and girls and not socialising, it turned out that Boris Johnson and his enablers in Downing Street were having multiple festive parties, while instructing us not to. The rule at the time was no parties. Asked about this, his spokesmodel assured us that all Covid safety rules were obeyed and kept repeating that line with every question they were asked, as though they could hypnotise us into believing them.

Last year, more than 100,000 people were fined a total of over £1m for breaking those rules but the Met Police leader announced she would not be investigating No 10 as the police do not now look into crimes that happened in the past, which came as great news to the criminal community.

In completely unfunny and very serious news, the bomb squad was alerted after a man arrived in the Accident and Emergency unit of Gloucestershire Royal Hospital after he "slipped and fell" onto a WWII anti-tank shell which became lodged in his rectum. The military collector claimed the armour-piercing munition was from his private arsenal.

Meanwhile, a group of 61 people who had shown up to see an Oasis tribute band called Noassis at the country's highest pub, Yorkshire's Tan Hill Inn were stranded there by a wonderwall of heavy snow blocking their exit. As one night turned into three, their plight became international news and a Blur tribute band was airlifted in and were immediately offered outside for a fight by fake Liam Gallagher.

The Tories lost the safe seat of North Shropshire, which they had held since the Cretaceous era, in a by-election caused the departure of their MP Owen Paterson who had been accused of egregious Toryism.

Bodger Johnson blamed the press for this loss, for reporting his lockdown busting parties and sleaze and cronyism and lies about Brexit and, well, everything.

If only the press had not called his failures failures, they'd be successes!

The Prime Minister was having such a wretched time that he appeared in public wearing a mask, so that you couldn't tell when he was lying, and in a late entry to the Peak Tory Award, there was news of the levelling up grants which was a pool of taxpayers' cash to be used for the purpose of helping those most in need, to be distributed to those in the poorer areas, so that they might catch up with the richer.

In what seems like the punchline to a joke, an actual Viscount, hereditary peer and ex-Conservative MP used a third of a million pounds of the levelling up grants to level the driveway to his £10m Tudor manor, set on 7,500 acres, on which he owned 114 houses, two pubs and a cricket green, in five villages.

It really doesn't get more Tory than that.

And as the year drew to a close, we ended it the same way we ended last year, by hoping that NEXT year is a lot better than this one.

Now the list. This is not a totally exhaustive list of what happened to us in 2021 but it's a pretty big one. If I have missed anything you wanted in, or added something you didn't, or made a mistake, then you can add that to the ever-growing list of life's little disappointments.

Thanks to everyone who contributed or just listened to the A-Z shows over Christmas on LBC.

A

Antifa - you know, the mob that stormed the US capitol on Jan 6!

Abdullah Abdul-Gawad, driver of the digger trying to free ship 'Ever Given' in Suez Canal.

Michael Apted, film director (d).

AUKUS caused a ruckus

Antibodies

Antigens

Alfresco No 10 "business meetings"

Virgil Abloh, American fashion designer (d)

Adele released new album

Jennifer Arcuri tells all about B Johnson

Australia won the T20 Cricket World Cup

Alpaca Geronimo put down despite campaign

Australian/UK trade deal, worth £1 per year per household

Michael Avenatti, anti-Trump lawyer gets 30 months in prison for attempted extortion of Nike

Azuma, cracks found on the Class 800 LNER trains

Ed Asner, actor (d)

Arwen, storm

David Amess, MP (d)

Atlanta Braves win World Series for 1st time since 1995

Alcohol consumption way up in lockdowns

Prince Andrew's ties to Jeffrey Epstein, Virginia Giuffre and Ghislaine Maxwell

Afghanistan disorderly exit of US & UK troops

Julian Assange appeals UK court's US extradition ruling

ABBA reunite for new album

Anti-vaxxers

Anti-maskers

Aten, 3000 year old city found, Egypt

Douglas Ankrah, bartender, creator of Pornstar Martini (d)

Amazon warehouse collapse in Illinois during tornado

Sergio Aguero retires from football with heart condition

Astro, musician, UB40 (d)

Artillery shell from man's personal arsenal had to be removed from man's personal a**e

Asymptomatic with Covid-19

Alpha (Kent) variant

Article 16, UK threatens EU re. N. Ireland protocol

Aung San Suu Kyi jailed after Myanmar coup

Abattoirs lack workers after Brexit/Covid

Avocados' environmental impact publicised

Algeria, last country to sell leaded petrol phases it out

A68, once world's largest iceberg, melts

Animal Rebellion, activists

Ant & Dec get ever so slightly political

Amber list countries (Covid travel restrictions)

Jake Angeli, "QAnon Shaman", jailed for part in Capital riot

Jake Angeli refuses to eat non-organic prison food

Magdalena Andersson, Swedish PM resigns after a few hours over budget defeat

Abydos, Egypt, world's oldest known beer factory unearthed

Arcadia empire sold, Top Shop, Burton's, Wallis, Dorothy Perkins, etc

Alba Party founded, led by Alex Salmond

Astrazeneca vaccine

Adverse reaction to vaccine

AI prosecutors developed in China, spot dissent with "97% accuracy"

Ahmaud Arbery, murdered by 3 white men, South Georgia (d)

April Ashley, model, trans activist (d)

Austrian brothel offers free sex for on-site vaccination

Anosmia, loss of sense of taste or smell, Covid symptoms

Amazon changes app logo after Hitler comparisons

Anagram: Delta and Omicron makes "media control"

Arts and design courses face 50% government funding cut

"Astronaut 001" title Richard Branson gives himself

Adele interviewer from Australia says he hadn't heard her album, apologises

B
James Bond film finally released

Lionel Blair, actor (d)

Aaron Banks, lost his case with HMRC over his donations to UKIP.

Steve Bray continues Brexit protest outside Parliament

Boris/Bodger/Bodge

Barbados becomes a Republic

Buttocks, England supporter puts lit flare there after drink and drugs bender

Boaty McBoatface robotic submarine on RRS Sir David Attenborough on Antarctica science mission

"Blah, blah, blah" Greta Thunberg's assessment of world leaders' climate change efforts

Beta variant

Barra, storm

Alec Baldwin, accidental shooting on the Rust movie set

"Bunny hugging" B Johnson mocks climate activists

"Bunny hugger", Greta Thunberg changes her Twitter profile name

Harold Bornstein, Donald Trump's personal physician (d)

Tony Blair's mullet lockdown hairstyle

Bo, Obama's dog (d)

Johnny Briggs, actor (d)

Butler secretly delivers £27,000 free organic food to B Johnson, paid for by Tory donor

John Bercow says B Johnson has 'only a nodding acquaintance with the truth'

John Bercow, ex-Tory MP defects to Labour

Batter – MCC's new PC name for batsman

Botoxed camels disqualified from Saudi beauty contest

Booster jabs

Bexley and Sidcup by-election held by Tory Party with much reduced majority

BBC gets new logo in rebrand

David Barclay, Telegraph co-owner (d)

Colin Bell, footballer (d)

Bernie's mittens, Sander's attire during Biden's inauguration

Dawn Butler, MP ejected from Commons for calling out B Johnson's lying

Brexit bonus yet to be felt

Denise Bryer, actor (d)

Rachel Blackmore, first female jockey to win Grand National

Beach handball, Norway women's team fined for not wearing bikini bottoms

Jeff Bezos in space

Richard Branson in space

Alex Beresford/Piers Morgan TV row

Belarus "hijacks" Ryanair plane with opposition journalist on board

Steve Bronski, singer (d)

Sean Bailey, Tory London mayoral candidate, party during lockdown allegation

Plan B (Covid)

Blue Origin, Jeff Bezos' interestingly shaped rocket

Border checks on island of Ireland

Border Force named Border Farce in media

Biden removes Trump's Diet Coke button from Oval Office

Bitcoin's energy use highlighted

Martin Bashir, BBC journalist accusations re. Princess Di interview etc

B.1.1.529 (Omicron variant)

Boat Race held on River Great Ouse due to closure of Hammersmith Bridge

Tony Bennett retires at 95

James Brokenshire, MP (d)

Leslie Bricusse, songwriter (d)

"Build Back Better" multi-national political slogan

Ian Botham made UK trade envoy to Australia

Brexit's gone badly say most people in poll on anniversary of leaving

Steve Bannon indicted for contempt re. Capital riot investigation

Philip Birch, founder Radio London (d)

Blackouts from storms

Bounce Back Loans fraud

Binman sacked for kicking head off snowman

Beavers reintroduced across UK

Gabriel Boric, elected President of Chile

Bronze Age treasures, many discoveries

Tony Bennett sets record as oldest person to release album of new material

Silvio Berlusconi announces bid for Italian presidency

Gordon Brown campaigns for 1st world to give vaccines to 3rd world

Bird flu, UK's largest ever outbreak

Joe Biden "breaks wind" in front of Camilla

Bottled water shortage, supply chain issues

Bookcases behind every at-home pundit on TV

Ashli Babbitt, Washington Capitol rioter shot (d)

Peter Bottomley, Tory MP says living on £82,000 a year is "really grim"

Bears, 3 napping in tree, officials close road to give them peace, Virginia

Boohoo buys Debenhams

Chris Barber, musician (d)

Brexit – government orders civil servants not to mention it

Bomb from man's "personal arsenal" removed from bottom after "trip"

Banana bread recipes top Google searches

Kay Burley suspended over Covid rule breaking by Sky News

Beano changes Spotty to Scotty, Fatty to Freddy

Sky Brown, GB's youngest ever Olympic medallist, skateboarding

Bilsdale transmitter fire deprives 1m of TV, radio in North East

C

COP26

Colin v Cuthbert the Caterpillar war, M&S and Aldi make similar cakes

Raul Castro steps down as Cuban Communist Party leader

Gerry Cottle, circus owner (d)

"Chatty Rat", No.10 leaker

Dominic Cummings' blog revelations re No10

Dominic Cummings' Select Committee evidence

Michael Collins, Apollo 11 astronaut (d)

Colosseum, Rome plans for new retractable floor

Ted Cruz, Texas senator goes to sunny Cancun while Texas freezes

Carrie Antoinette, name given to demanding wife of B Johnson

Eric Carle, Author of The Very Hungry Caterpillar (d)

"Cowardly Wet Noodle" Description of Bodger by Jennifer Arcuri

Champ, Biden's dog (d)

Gina Coladangelo. Matt Handcock's lover

John Challis, actor (d)

CO2 Shortage.

Clown shortage in Northern Ireland due to lockdowns

Coldplay announce no more albums from 2025.

Covid-19

Conservatorship, Britney Spears' ends

Cancel Culture

Culture wars

Chelsea FC win Champions League

Cocaine, found everywhere in Parliament

Stella Creasy, MP reprimanded for bringing her baby into the House of Commons

Cat filter turns lawyer into feline during Zoom meeting

Daniel Craig appears in his final Bond film

Derek Chauvin, US police officer convicted for killing George Floyd.

Storm Christoph

Piers Corbyn arrested on suspicion of encouraging arson

Candle factory collapse in Kentucky during tornado

Cheese and wine "business meetings" at No10 during lockdown

Angelique Coetzee, S. African doctor who raised alarm re. Omicron variant

John Chilcot, chair of Iraq Inquiry (d)

Maureen Cleave, journalist (d)

Clive Sinclair, inventor/entrepreneur (d)

Cricket racism scandal

China's crypto-currency crackdown

Cat burglar, feline in NZ steals bong, drugs, nickers and steel toed boots

Co-morbidities, re. Covid infection outcome

Contact tracing

Corruption allegations against government

Capital Hill coup attempt

Covid passes

Cuttlefish, first evidence of animal whose memory does not fade with age

Contactless card limit increased

Cashless society draws closer

Simon Case, civil servant quits No10 party probe after admitting he also broke rules

Cosmos 1408, Russian spy satellite destroyed by Russian rocket

David Cameron, Greensill lobbying controversy

Jonathan "Jono" Coleman, DJ & TV presenter (d)

Terry Cooper, footballer (d)

Cronyism

Crops dying in the fields due to lack of workers due to Brexit & virus

Chesham and Amersham by-election lost by Tories, won by Lib Dems

Wayne Cousins, Met Police officer convicted of murder of Sarah Everard

Samantha Cristoforetti, E S A astronaut has Barbie released in her image

Andrew Cuomo, NY Governor resigns over harassment llegations

Chris Cuomo, CNN host fired for helping brother Andrew

Peter Corby, inventor of Corby trouser press (d)

"Convival fraternal spirit" Mogg's reason why maskless Tories won't catch virus

Caravaggio, suspected Old Master almost sold at auction for £1,300

Chelsea Flower Show postponed for first time in 108 year history

Chick Corea, musician (d)

Covidiots

Phil Chen, musician (d)

Naomi Campbell has first baby

Therese Coffey DWP minister defends Universal Credit cut

Therese Coffey, Tory Conference karaoke choice "We're having the time of our lives"

Crown symbol on pint glasses, "Brexit bonus"

Eric Clapton's vaccine sceptic conspiracy theories

Circuit breaker lockdowns

Culling pigs due to lack of abattoir workers due to Brexit

"Captain hindsight" Johnson flails at Starmer

Clarkson's Farm, talked about TV show

Geoffrey Cox MP's multiple jobs

Cash for honours

Check-out free stores

Canada, mass child graves found at Roman Catholic schools

Chumocracy, government accused of cronyism

Princess Charlene of Monaco suffering from "exhaustion"

Cumbre Vieja volcano erupts, La Palma

Covid passports

Camels enhanced with botox banned from Saudi beauty contest

Cold War Steve, political artist/satirist

Mark Cavendish wins 4 stages of Tour de France, equals record

Eric Clapton, lockdown sceptic work with Van Morrison

Cookies pop-up consent on websites

D

De-platforming

Dinghy crossings of refugees from France

Cressida Dick, Met Police chief refuses to investigate No10 over Partygate

Donny's diapers, odd padding in Trump's trouser area

Frederik Willem de Klerk, Ex-President of S Africa (d)

Ted Dexter, cricketer (d)

Domestic flight tax reduction announced by Sunak in run-up to Cop26

Mark Drakeford, Welsh First Minister announces Covid curbs

Doxxing, JK Rowland's address posted on social media re. trans row

Delta variant

Paul Dacre, Johnson attempts and fails to install him as head of Ofcom

Tom Daley knits

Tom Daley wins first Olympic gold medal with Matty Lee

David, Edinburgh Zoo's oldest chimp (d)

Downing St briefing room cost £2.6m, used to show Bond film to B Johnson

Debenhams closes

Olympia Dukakis, actor (d)

Bob Dole, US politician (d)

DART, NASA's anti-asteroid spacecraft launched

Dover Lifeboat crew booed by anti-migrants

Gianluigi Donnarumma, Italy goalkeeper saves 2 England penalties, Euro 2020

Darius, world's biggest rabbit stolen in Worcestershire

Nadine Dorries kicked out of Tory WhatsApp group by Steve Baker

Stuart Damon, actor (d)

Vitamin D, advised to take for Covid protection

Richard Donner, film maker (d)

Diet Coke, Trump's Oval Office button removed by Biden

"Donnez-moi un break" Johnson responds to French reaction to Aukus deal

Dinosaur embryo found in egg fossil

Joan Didion, writer (d)

Dartmore Rail Line reinstated

Dognapping

Dubai ruler, biggest divorce case in UK history, £500m settlement

Doomscrolling

Princess Di statue unveiled

Fred Dinenage announces retirement from TV news post

Decolonising

Dressing up box, Johnson pretends to do other's jobs for photos

Robert Durst, "The Jinx" documentary subject, convicted of murder

Jack Dorsey, Twitter founder resigns

Daft Punk announce retirement

John Dawes, rugby player (d)

Dr Seuss Enterprises withdraws 6 titles due to racial stereotypes

Dustin Diamond, actor (d)

Dog, lurcher, walks with limp out of sympathy with injured owner

E

Ever Given got stuck in Suez Canal

Extinction Rebellion, activists

Sarah Everard killed by Met Police officer (d)

Sarah Everard protest broken up by Met Police

E10 fuel introduced

Mark Eden, actor (d)

Graeme Edge, musician Moody Blues (d)

E-learning, home schooling

Euro 2020 held in 2021, England lose to Italy on penalties

Exams cancelled in schools

Elephants evolve tuskless due to poaching

European Super League plans quashed

Lee Elder, golfer (d)

Einsteinium, researchers reveal chemical secrets of mysterious element

E-scooters

Alber Elbaz, fashion designer (d)

Eurovision Song Contest, UK-nul points

Energy prices

Duke of Edinburgh (d)

Spencer Elden, man who was baby on Nirvana's Never Mind album sues for sexual exploitation

Don Everly, musician (d)

Natalie Elphicke, Tory MP criticises Marcus Rashford over missed penalty & backtracks

Natalie Elphicke praises food banks, the use of which is up 400% under Tories

Christian Eriksen collapses Euro 2020

Exponential growth of Omicron variant

Epidemiologists

Earthshot Prize, environmental solutions invited to planet's problems

Epsilon variant

Erasmus student exchange programme closed to Britons due to Brexit

Exports down with EU

Clarissa Eden, wife of PM Anthony (d)

El Salvador first country to accept Bitcoin as legal tender

Everydays: The First 5000 Days NFT artwork sells for $69.3m

Linda Evangelista sues cosmetic surgery co. for $50m

Europa, Jupiter moon confirmed to hold water

Pee Wee Ellis, musician (d)

Nathan Evans, postman turned sea shanty star

F

Fatty from Beano renamed Freddy

Florida, Surfside condominium collapse

"Forgive me" B Johnson loses place in CBI speech

David Frost resigns post as EU negotiator

Nigel Farage quits politics

Nigel Farage available for birthday shout-out videos

Nigel Farage US comeback tour flops

Fox News sued by Dominion voting machines over allegations of election fraud

FA charged by UEFA over fans' conduct at Euro 2020 final

France bans sale of inflatables to deter migrant crossings

Ron Flowers, footballer (d)

Robert Fyfe, actor (d)

Furlough scheme ends

Fishing industry decimated despite Brexit promises

Fish are "better and happier" as they are "now British" after Brexit: Rees-Mogg

Fishing licences for France, UK climbdown

Facebook changes company name to Meta

Facebook and subsidiaries' temporary blackout

F**k overtakes bl**dy as UK's most popular swear word

Foreign Office relaxes as Afghanistan crumbles

Fuel shortage

Fuel suppliers fail

Arlene Foster, DUP leader resigns after letters of no confidence sent

Fake news

Food banks

Friends TV reunion

Farfarout discovered, most distant known object in solar system

"Freedom Day", Johnson calls it too soon

Freddy, world's tallest dog (d)

Dawn Foster, journalist (d)

Flags, government break out the Union Jacks

Larry Flint, publisher (d)

Fagradalsfjall volcano, longest eruption for 50 years in Iceland

French workers now allowed to eat lunch at their desks

Flatulence, Joe Biden allegedly farts at COP26

Folic acid added to all non-wholemeal wheat flour

Forest fires, Australia, California, Canada etc

Professor Neil "Lockdown" Fergusson

Formula One World Championship, Max Verstappen race controversy

Festival of Brexit renamed 'UNBOXED: Creativity in the UK'

Face masks

The Faces reform and record new material

Floods

Flat renovation, B Johnson's claims he didn't know payee rubbished

Paul "Pen" Farthing's animal sanctuary airlift, Afghanistan

Foreign aid cut

Forest Green Rovers becomes world's first carbon-neutral football club

Nigel Farage in Cameo video messaging service

Nigel Farage tricked into recording pro-IRA messages

Facebook, most shared post was of Trump's plummeting net worth

France to ban short-haul domestic flights where train alternatives exist

Fake arm, Italian tries to dodge vaccine

Cameron Ford of Insulate Britain v Mike Graham on TalkRadio, Ford wins

"Following the science" government refrain

Siegfried Fischbacher, magician (d)

"Following the rules", government refrain when they weren't

Facebook whistleblower, Francis Haugen, urges regulation to reduce harm

Andy Fordham, darts player (d)

Mark Francois self-publishes Brexit account after rejection from "remoaner" publishers

Maya Forstater wins tribunal over "gender critical" beliefs

G

Gaslighting

Michael Gove and Sarah Vine announce divorce

Michael Gove, "I love dancing", spotted throwing odd shapes in Aberdeen disco

Lou Grant, actor (d)

G7 summit in Cornwall

Gas shortage

Gold wallpaper, Johnson's flat refurbishment

Jimmy Greaves, footballer (d)

Glacier melt

Geronimo the alpaca (d)

GB News launches

Get Boosted Now, text message sent Boxing Day

G7, Cornwall, awkward group photos

Global warming

Amanda Gorman, poet at Biden's inauguration

Bill and Melinda Gates divorce

Gold statue of Trump at CPAC co-designed by Mexican, made in China

Greek alphabet used for naming variants

Glastonbury online event

Goats, Old Irish, employed to graze around Dublin to prevent wildfires

Charles Grodin, actor (d)

Garrick Club, Johnson takes jet from COP26 to dine with mates

Genesis, final tour

Nikki Grahame, TV personality (d)

Greenwashing, companies' falsify eco credentials

Good Law Project hold government to account

Gender neutral passports, Supreme Court disallows

GameStop shares surge due to Reddit investors

Glue, used by Insulate Britain for sticking faces to M25

Nancy Griffith, singer (d)

Green list countries for travel

"Green steel", Swedish company ships first batch

Gulf of Mexico, "eye of fire" after underwater gas leak

General Sherman, world's largest tree wrapped in foil due to wildfires

Virginia Giuffre, accuses Ghislaine Maxwell and Prince Andrew

Sarah Green, elected Lib Dem MP for Chesham and Amersham

Gallows erected during Capital riot, Washington DC

Abdulrazak Gurnah wins Nobel prize for literature

GitHub Copilot, AI programmer aids code writing

Rudy Giuliani sued by Georgia poll workers over fraud allegations

Get Back, Beatles TV documentary

"Rainbow" George, regular LBC caller, Hampstead eccentric (d)

GP appointments hard to get

Graphs and charts re. virus

Zac Goldsmith loans Johnson Marbella villa linked to offshore tax havens

"Guided by the science" government refrain

Greyscale, rail website tribute to Prince Philip hampers visually impaired

Nicholas Gage, Tory Lord uses £330k from Levelling Up fund to pave own driveway

Greensill Capital lobbying scandal, David Cammeron

Mike Graham, TalkRadio host insists you can grow concrete

Geordie Greg steps down as editor Daily Mail

Giant millipede, largest fossil found, 9 feet long, Northumberland

Gin, light-up bottles spat between M&S and Aldi

Greece fines elderly vaccine refusers 100 Euros per month

Gran Canaria tourists having sex risk dunes nature reserve

Glaswegians force Immigration Enforcement to release two asylum seekers

Keith Gill, trader invests in GameStop, followers cause huge spike

Global Health Insurance Card, reciprocal health cover UK/ EU

H

Matt Hancock caught on CCTV canoodling

Hancock resigned says Johnson

Hancock fired says Johnson

HGV driver shortage

Hong Kong universities remove Tiananmen Sq massacre monuments

Sarah Harding, singer (d)

"Happy fish", Rees-Mogg's preposterous pronouncement

Handforth Parish Council Zoom meeting row goes viral

Her Game Too, anti-sexist football campaign

Sally Ann Howes, actor (d)

Dusty Hill, musician, ZZ Top (d)

Lewis Hamilton loses F1 crown

Herd immunity

Marvin Hagler, boxer (d)

Hotel quarantine

Heathrow drop-off charge, £5

Halyna Hutchins, cinematographer shot on Alex Baldwin movie set (d)

Highly transmissible variant

HS2 Eastern Leg cancelled

Huntsman spider crawls on health minister during TV briefing, Australia

Ron Hill, runner, clothing entrepreneur (d)

Haiti President, Jovenel Moise, assassinated (d)

Dennis Hutchings, ex-soldier on trial for Troubles shooting (d)

Ham sandwich, driver's lunch confiscated at Dutch border after Brexit

Harriet Harman, mother of the house, announces retirement from politics

Heat domes cause wildfires, deaths

HOGO, the hassle of going out

Highway 9, Insulate Britain activists jailed

Heat pumps, eco alternative to boilers

Halogen bulbs banned from sale

Heinz Christmas dinner in a can

Bill Harkin, Glastonbury Pyramid stage designer (d)

Hospitalisations

Hospitality sector suffers

Bernard Haitink, conductor (d)

Roger Hunt, footballer (d)

Hornsea 2, world's biggest offshore wind farm produces first power

House price increase

Hairdressers shut

Kamala Harris, first woman to get presidential powers while Biden hospitalised

Hands. Face. Space. new government slogan

Hurricane Ida causes deadly tornados in six US states

Henley Royal Regatta allows women to wear trousers

Hong Kong's first elections under anti-democratic Chinese rules

Human rights under attack in UK

Hospitals, 40 new ones promised

Hospital management ordered to count refurbs as new hospitals

Hospital staff get no real terms pay rise despite 2 years of Covid response

Hypersonic missiles launched from China, stuns world

Alan Holmes, musician (d)

Hal Holbrook, actor (d)

"He's doing his best" Johnson's fans defend him

Alan Hart, former head of BBC Sport/BBC1 (d)

Laurel Hubbard, first openly trans woman to compete at Olympics

Line of Duty, talked about TV show

Harry and Meghan's Oprah interview

Harry and Meghan's shoeless b&w tree picture

Harry and Meghan still focus of tabloids' ire

Home schooling

David Henderson jailed for flight that killed Emiliano Sala, David Ibbotson

Highway Code rule changes for cyclists and drivers

Elizabeth Holmes, CEO Theranos, near $1bn blood test fraudster on trial

Alan Hawkshaw, composer (d)

I

Insulate Britain's road blocking campaign

Irish Sea bridge, B Johnson's plans rejected

IR35, HMRC rule change for self-employed

Imports down with EU

Isolating

Ray Illingworth, cricketer (d)

Import checks, Brexit

"Idiots", Tony Blair's description of anti-vaxxers

Interest rate rise, first in three years

Independent SAGE

Inflation

Immigration

Ingenuity, NASA's Mars helicopter's first flight

Irish border

"Institutional corruption", Met Police accusation

Ivermectin, antiparasitic taken as alternative Covid treatment

Infection rates

Incels

Infuenza rates drop sharply

Immunity from Covid

Imperial measurements, Brexit "bonus"

Inspiration4, world's first all-civilian mission to orbit Earth

Ikea buys 11,000 acres of land in Georgia to prevent development

International Bar Association's Human Rights Institute evacuate 370 people from Afghanistan

Idaho gets record 30 inches of snow

Iran-US nuclear talks

India-UK trade deal sought by Johnson

India left off red list of countries despite Indian variant

Italian cable car crash, Stresa-Alpino-Mottarone

"I'm not a cat", lawyer tries to remove Zoom filter

"Is everything OK?" reporter to Johnson after CBI speech mess

Ice block falls from one airborne plane onto another smashing windscreen

Iranian nuclear scientist Mohsen Fakhrizadeh killed by remote control weapon

Independent SAGE, government advisors

Laura Ingraham, Fox News host recreates "Who's on first" routine

Iel, gender-neutral pronoun included in Le Petit Robert French dictionary

Ig Nobel Prize for economics for study on link: corruption of politicians and obesity

Icelandair passenger tests positive for Covid, self-isolates in toilet for 5 hour flight

J

Boris Johnson refuses to wear a mask in hospital, Commons, next to David Attenborough...

Boris Johnson weds Carrie Symonds in Catholic church despite 2 divorces

Boris Johnson's holiday in Spain paid for by someone else

Boris Johnson's flat refurb paid for by someone else

Boris Johnson's organic food bill paid for by someone else

Boris Johnson says Britons should not rely on handouts

Stanley Johnson accused of sexual harassment

Stanley Johnson applies for French citizenship as son "gets Brexit done"

Judicial Review Bill, risks narrowing public's access to justice

Jethro, comedian (d)

JP Morgan protest at Cop26 for being world's largest fossil fuel financier

Joey Jordison, musician, Slipknot (d)

Just-in-time manufacturing process upended due to Brexit & virus

Jingle Jabs vaccine promotion

Sajid Javid, SuperSaj, takes over as Health Secretary

Johnnie Johnson, last surviving Dambuster reaches 100 years old

Jersey electricity cut threatened by France over fishing rights

John Lewis stores close

Jerrycan sales spike over fuel panic buying

Jesus wants you to get jabbed implies B Johnson

Sasha Johnson, equal rights activist shot

Rick Jones, children's TV presenter (d)

James Webb Telescope $10bn instrument launched

Jaeger bought by M&S

Christopher Geidt, Johnson's ethics advisor clears PM over flat refurb

Christopher Geidt, Johnson's ethics advisor misled by Johnson, allegedly

Andy Jassy new CEO of Amazon

Tom Jones, oldest man to top album charts

Michael Jordan, NBA star, donates $10 million for new medical clinics in N Carolina.

Joint Committee on Vaccination and Immunisation

Joint Biosecurity Centre

Juno, search & rescue dog missing, found after 6 days

"Just setting up my twtrr", tweet by founder Jack Dorsey sells as NFT, $2.9m

Ron Jeremy, porn star sex assault allegations

Jezero Crater, Perseverance Rover's landing site, Mars

"Jingle jabs", Xmas vaccine push

K

Kill the Bill campaign re. Police and Crime Bill

Kentucky hit by tornados

Kentucky, two babies rescued in bath after tornados

Laura Kuenssberg announces step down from BBC political editorship

Kermit joke falls flat in B Johnson's rambling UN climate speech

"Kermit permit" driver's dub Kent Access Permit after Brexit border shambles

Kenneth Kaunda, ex President of Zambia (d)

Knee, the taking of at football, first booed, then applauded

Knee, the taking of, solo boycott of England games by Tory MP Lee Anderson

Larry King, TV host (d)

Kabul falls to the Taliban

Sadiq Khan wins second term as London Mayor

Ray Kennedy, footballer (d)

Keith, kleptomaniac cat steals bong, drugs, knickers, shoes in New Zealand

KPMG UK boss quits after telling staff to stop moaning re. pandemic working conditions

Kids Company directors win case re. mismanagement

Kew Gardens accused of being woke re. signs on plants role in slave trade

Yaphet Kotto, actor (d)

Nick Kamen, Levi's model, singer (d)

Kingspan, Grenfell Tower cladding company sponsors Mercedes F1

Kingspan sponsorship of Mercedes F1 ended after backlash

John F Kennedy assassination documents released

Captain Kirk boldly goes where many men have been before

Knitting, Tom Daley at Olympics

King Crimson's final show, Robert Fripp says "moved from sound to silence"

Kidney donated from Israeli man to Arab woman after she waits 10 years

Jurgen Klopp calls out Trump, Johnson, Farage on leadership

Brendan Kennelly, poet (d)

"Kung Fuel Fighting" Sun headline re. forecourt fight during petrol shortage

Laura & Jason Kenny most successful ever GB Olympians

Kenton, Devon, church bells stopped by one complaint after 121 years

L

Leaded petrol eradicated from world

"Let's go Brandon", journalist's misreport of chant "F**K Joe Biden" goes viral

Janice Long, broadcaster (d)

La Palma volcano erupts

Alan Lancaster, musician, Status Quo (d)

Lockdowns

Long Covid

Labour Party leads polls after Tory Partygate, sleaze, cronyism, cash for honours etc

George Linnane rescued by 250 cavers from Ogof Ffynnon Ddu cave, Wales

LadBaby set chart record for fourth consecutive Xmas number 1

Doreen Lofthouse, Fisherman's Friend entrepreneur (d)

Sean Lock, comedian (d)

Lilibet, Harry & Meghan's name for baby

Lab leak theory of virus

Lies, many told by government

"Liar", Dawn Butler ejected from Commons for description of B Johnson

Leicester City win FA Cup

Lady Gaga's dog walker Ryan Fischer shot

Dilip Kumar, actor (d)

Laughing gas, Priti Patel orders review, promises "tough" action

Rush Limbaugh, radio host (d)

G. Gordon Liddy, Watergate conspirator (d)

Longwave, ship takes last export of coal from Tyneside

Levelling up, government promise

Princess Latifa claims father, Dubai ruler, holding her hostage

Leasehold Reform Bill gives homeowners new rights

Lateral flow test

Liberal Democrats' by-election wins

Lobbying scandal

Lulu Lytle, interior designer of Johnson's flat refurb

Low Traffic Neighbourhoods

Land Rover carries Prince Philip's coffin

Mike Lindell, the My Pillow guy spends $25m on false Trump election claims

Ursula von der Leyen, President of European Commission

Lucifer, more popular baby's name than Nigel

Llanfairpwllgwyngyllgogerychwyrndrobwllllantysiliogogogoch name-checked by Liam Dutton in TV weather forecast gets 57m views on YouTube

M

Angela Merkel, German Chancellor steps down after 16 years

Marble Arch Mount attraction opens and closes

Elon Musk, crypto, space, tax, shares, world's richest...

Freddy Marks, TV presenter Rainbow (d)

Meghan still enemy number one to UK tabloids

Benjamin Monk, PC jailed for death of ex-footballer Dalian Atkinson

Migrants' crossings from France

Migrants, 27 die in Channel crossing disaster

Les McKeown, singer, Bay City Rollers (d)

Ghislaine Maxwell found guilty at trial

Captain Tom Moore, fundraiser for NHS charities (d)

Thomas Massie, Rep. issues Xmas family photo with military weapons days after Michigan school shooting

Lionel Messi leaves FC Barcelona for PSG

Misogyny, D Raab thinks it means abuse against women or men

Helen McCrory, actor (d)

Gerry Marsden, musician, Gerry and the Pacemakers (d)

Mittens, Bernie Sanders' Biden inauguration accessories go viral

Major, Biden's dog's biting incidents

Mummies, Pharaohs Golden Parade, Cairo, Egypt

Bernie Madoff, ran largest Ponzi scheme in history (d)

Max Mosley, ex-president of FIA motor sport body (d)

Paul Mitchell, butler who delivered B Johnson's free Daylesford food

Walter Mondale former VP of USA (d)

John McAfee, software designer (d)

Abhimanyu Mishra, 12years 4 months old, youngest chess grandmaster

Maria Mendiola, singer, Baccara (d)

Samuel Mulligan, restaurant burglar gets drunk, still asleep when police arrive

Milkshakes, McDonald's runs out

Martinis, Queen gives up her daily sharpener

Darrell Meekcom, bucket list: moons speed camera, arrested

Midas, kitten born with 4 ears, Turkey

Piers Morgan departs Good Morning Britain after Meghan row

Met Police branded "institutionally corrupt" by inquiry

Meghan Markle wins privacy case against Mail on Sunday

Meta, new name for Facebook parent company

Metaverse, Facebook's Zuckerberg's name for virtual world

Emmanuel Macron, French President calls Johnson a clown

Mixed messages, government's virus advice

Nicki Minaj claims vaccine swelled cousin's friend's testicles

Manchester City win Premier League

M25 halted by Insulate Britain

MOD secret papers left at bus stop in Kent

Phil McCann, BBC TV reporter covers petrol shortage

Moderna vaccine

Masks

Malta legalises cannabis for personal use, European first

Marijuana, legal in Malta, change coming across Europe in 2022

Michael Masi, F1 Race Director, Hamilton/Verstappen controversy

Mars Oxygen In-Situ Resource Utilization Experiment, creates oxygen on Mars

Thomas "Mensi" Mensforth, musician (d)

Marmite shortage, supply of yeast issues

Iris Mohamedy, 86, united with online lover, 35, on This Morning TV show

Munch revealed to have written "Can only have been painted by a madman" on The Scream

Mathematical modelling re. virus

Moonflower rare cactus blooms for first time in the UK

Magawa, bomb detecting rat retires, Cambodia

Morris dancers ditch blackface after 500 years

John Miles, musician (d)

Mice plague, Australia

Mammoth graveyard 200,000 years old found near Swindon

Kylie Minogue moves back to Australia

mRNA vaccines

Microchip shortage causes 2nd hand car prices to rise

Malian woman gives birth to nine babies

John Madden, US football coach (d)

"Murder Hornets", Asian wasps invade USA, attack honey bee hives

Norm Macdonald, comedian (d)

Princess Mako of Japan says media caused her PTSD

Madagascar, climate change-induced famine

Helen Morgan, Lib Dem MP for N Shropshire, wins Tory safe seat

Princess Mako of Japan loses royal status after marrying a commoner

Marsh family, singing videos go viral

McDonald's apologises after snail found in burger

Maneskin, Eurovision winner denies cocaine use during show

Myanmar ambassador locked out of embassy, London

Van Morrison, lockdown sceptic work with Eric Clapton

Elon Musk announces $100m prize for carbon capture inventions

Microchip shortage

Miami condo collapse

Jackie Mason, comedian (d)

Charlie Mullins, Pimlico Plumbers boss "no jab, no job" policy

Charlie Mullins says he hasn't had the vaccine

John Morgan, musician, Wurzels (d)

Paul McCartney's bass guitar breaks auction record $471,900

N

NHS backlogs

Nationality and Borders Bill, immigration and anti-human rights bill

Newcastle Utd sold by Mike Ashley to Saudi Arabia PIF

Navy loses £100m jet over side of HMS Queen Elizabeth

The Netherlands, Christmas lockdown over Omicron wave

Nord Stream 2 Russian gas pipeline construction completed

Norwegian Xmas tree gift criticised

"Next slide please" virus briefing refrain

Mike Nesmith, musician, The Monkees (d)

Ted Nugent, rocker calls Covid a scam, catches Covid

James Newman, represents UK in Eurovision, nul points

"No rules were broken" government mantra re. Partygate

No Time To Die, Bond movie released

Nick Fletcher, Tory MP says female Dr Who turns boys to crime

"Nanny's home-made marmalade" Mogg's preference to Weetabix & beans

Natural gas wholesale prices

Nowzad, Afghanistan animal charity airlift

Gary Neville calls out Johnson as "worst kind of leader"

Nightingale hospitals closed

National Insurance, 10% rise announced

NHS nurses' pay rise to be wiped out by NI rise

Non-fungible token, virtual art sold

Andrew Neil sets up GB News, leaves shortly thereafter

Nobel Peace Prize winners: Maria Ressa and Dmitry Muratov

Mick Norcross, actor (d)

Kit Malthouse tells GMB he doesn't know where PM is, while meters away

Paddy Moloney, musician (d)

Mother in India names twins 'Corona' and 'Covid'

Newcastle Utd asks fans to stop wearing tea towels celebrating Saudi takeover

NASA's Double Asteroid Redirection Test, planetary defence craft launched

Xavier Novell, RC bishop resigns over love for satanic erotic novelist

Northern Line extension to Battersea and Nine Elms opens

Nightingale "surge hubs" set up

New Year's Eve, warmest on record

Ndakasi, Congo's famous gorilla (d)

Nu, WHO skips Greek letter for Covid variant name, homophone "new"

O

Oprah Winfrey interviews Harry and Meghan

2020 Olympics takes place in 2021

Omicron

Ofgem fuel price cap

Online GP appointments

"One Britain One Nation", "patriotic" school song

Tom O'Connor, comedian (d)

Barak Obama, virus forces scale back of 60th birthday party

Omnishambles, government's various travails

Ostritch extract used to highlight virus in Covid masks

Oven-ready deal still cooking

Beldina Odenyo Onassis, Heir of the Cursed, musician (d)

Oxygen shortage in hospitals

Only Fans site announces then reverses sex ban

Only Fools and Horses van sells for £36,000 at auction

Bob Odenkirk, actor has heart attack

Otters attack British man in Singapore, 26 bites in 10 seconds

P

Peanut Butter and Jelly, name of turkeys pardoned by Biden in Thanksgiving tradition

Petrol shortage, panic queuing

Poland-Belarus border migrant crisis

Edwin Poots, short-lived DUP leader

Police, Crime, Sentencing and Courts Bill, attempt to criminalise protest

Peppa Pig, B Johnson rambles at CBI address

Poland fights with EU re. gay rights

Post Office Horizon IT scandal

Plymouth shooting, 5 killed, plus shooter

"Princess Nut Nuts", name given to PM's wife by adversaries

Potato, world's biggest grown in New Zealand, 7.8 kilograms

Pfizer vaccine

Power cuts after Storm Arwen

Lee "Scratch" Perry, record producer (d)

Owen Paterson lobbying scandal

Owen Paterson suspended

Owen Paterson suspension opposed by Tories

Owen Paterson suspension opposition Tory U-turn, resigns

Priti Patel wants asylum seekers to be sent for processing to Albania, Albania refuses

Pandora Papers offshore tax haven data release

Jen Psaki, Biden's press secretary

Priti Patel disinvited to French Channel crisis meeting

Priti Patel calls on France to take Channel crossing migrants back

Partygate at Number 10

Proud Boys, armed ding-a-lings

David Perry, taxi driver thwarts Liverpool Women's Hospital bomber

Post Office, wrongly convicted workers have names cleared

Trevor Peacock, actor (d)

Perseverance, Mars rover

Plan B, Covid response

Pints of Champagne, Liz Truss promises Brexit bonus

PCR tests, Johnson says to get one

PCR tests unavailable

Katie Price flips car while drunk and disqualified

Vilfred Pareto, B Johnson cites economist as inspiration, as did Mussolini

Gabby Petito murder case

Pig cull due to abattoir staff shortages

Percy Pig sweets exports hit by Brexit red tape

Potato Head drops the "Mr" in gender-neutral rebrand

Pingdemic, disruption due to many testing positive for Covid

Private jet used by Johnson to get to dinner from Cop26 climate talks

PPE pollution from discarded masks

Nicola Pagett, actor (d)

Colin Pitchfork, murderer released, then recalled to prison

"Pilot scheme", why Johnson claimed he didn't have to isolate

Budge Patty, tennis player (d)

Dolly Parton sings rewrite of Jolene as "Vaccine, vaccine..."

Christopher Plummer, actor (d)

Chris Packham v fox hunters

Penguin, rare Antarctic Adelie accidentally travels 3000km to NZ

Melvin van Peebles, actor (d)

Lloyd Price, singer (d)

Paper money completely replaced by polymer as new £50 introduced

"Plague island" Europeans' name for GB after virus surge

Pensions triple lock suspended

Postman in Falkirk leaves injured OAP in snow because "too knackered" to help

Puberty blockers, court rules under 16's can use treatment

Victoria Prentis, Fisheries Minister didn't read Brexit bill, as she was on nativity trail

Mike Pence VP certifies Biden as President despite pressure

Sinead O'Connor confirms retirement from music industry, again

"Pigcasso", pig painter sells work for £20,000

"Poop tomatoes" found by sewage affected rivers, Kent

Prince's white dove, Divinity, "ambient singer" on Arboretum (d)

Q

QAnon believers await JFK Jr.'s return in Dallas on JFK assassination anniversary

Quidditch players distance themselves from creator JK Rowling

Quiz, Johnson claims lockdown busting party was just a quiz

Quicksand, 3 teens trapped, rescued, Nottinghamshire quarry

Quotas, fishing row with French

Queuing for petrol, vaccines, tests, border control at Heathrow, etc

Quarantini, alcohol consumption up in lockdown

Quangos, bonfire of promised by G Osborne judged a failure

Quitting, workers resign bad jobs in great numbers after lockdowns

Quality Street announces new flavour: Creme Caramel Crisp

Queen sits alone due to social distancing rules at Philip's funeral

QR codes replace menus and ordering at the bar

Quarantine

Qualification rounds for Qatar World Cup

Quantitative easing wound down

Queen's Xmas speech dubbed most personal

R

Red list countries (Covid related travel bans)

Red tape, no bonfire on Brexit, just more of it

"Road map" B Johnson's "plan" for Covid

Marcus Rashford shows government what caring looks like

Gloria Richardson, activist (d)

Angela Rayner, Labour MP calls Tories "scum", apologises

"Read them and understand them" Handforth Parish Council row

Dominic Raab denies paddle-boarding while Kabul fell as "sea was closed"

Emma Raducanu wins 2021 US Open women's singles title

JK Rowling ahead in Guardian Person of the Year poll, poll cancelled

Kyle Rittenhouse, Kenosha shooter, found not guilty

Dominic Raab declines to cut holiday short during Afghanistan evacuation

Mick Rock, photographer (d)

Paul Ritter, actor (d)

R number, infection rate of Covid

Rihanna becomes billionaire from stake in cosmetics company

RNLI booed by anti-migrants

Refurbishments of Number 10 and who paid

Ring doorbell, judge rules invade privacy of Oxford neighbour

Cecil Rhodes statue in Oriel College gets plaque "contextualising" imperialist

Remote learning due to lockdowns

Dominic Raab says police don't investigate things that took place a year ago

Donald Rumsfeld, US politician (d)

Richard Rogers, architect (d)

Tanya Roberts, actor (d)

Ben Roberts, actor (d)

Barry Ryan, singer (d)

Register of members' interests, second jobs scandal

Resignations, "The Great Resignation", 1 in 4 planning to quit their jobs

Racism at the Palace, Harry and Meghan allegations

RHS opens Bridgewater, "Europe's biggest horticultural project"

Rollout of vaccine

Azeem Rafiq, cricket racism accusations

Angela Richardson's Twitter attack on the wrong James O'Brien

Albert Roux, chef (d)

Cristiano Ronaldo returns to Manchester United

Rewilding projects

Jacob Rees-Mogg fails to declare £6m cheap loan from own company

S

Sleaze, government behaviour

Cleo Smith says "My name is Cleo" on being found in Australia after 2 weeks missing

William Shatner, Admiral James T. Kirk, boldly goes where many men have gone before

Sewage, untreated, allowed by govt to be pumped into rivers and sea

Travis Scott Astroworld concert tragedy

Olaf Scholz, new Chancellor of Germany

North Shropshire by-election, Tory lose ultra-safe seat, Lib Dems win

Shock G, rapper (d)

Space telescope, James Webb, most powerful, launches

Salt Bae, restaurant serves gold leaf covered steak at £1450

Keir Starmer fails to cut through

Succession, lauded TV show

Squid Game, lauded TV show

Serpent, lauded TV show

Allegra Stratton, PM's press secretary laughs over "partygate" question

Allegra Stratton cries on resigning post as PM's press secretary

Supply chain issues

Keir Starmer thrown out of Bath pub in lockdown row

Ole Gunnar Solskjaer let go as Manchester United manager

South African woman lies about birth of 10 babies

Iain Duncan Smith hit on head with a traffic cone

Roaming charges return after Brexit

Rochdale fans raise £10k for statue of superfan David Clough

Scorpion plague as they shelter in homes from storms, Egypt

Space tourism

Shortages, petrol, food, Covid tests, microchips, oxygen, etc

Sausage Wars, Brexit

Bruce Springsteen sells entire music catalogue for $500m

Una Stubbs, actor (d)

Nicola Sturgeon celebrates SNP election win

Supermarket trolley, broken, Cummings' description of Johnson

Suez Canal got blocked

Jim Steinman, composer, producer (d)

Staycations

Gareth Southgate takes England to Euro finals

Selfridges sold to Thai-Austrian firms for £4bn

Rishi Sunak offers £6,000 grants to struggling businesses, same as per day rate to consultants

Rishi Sunak releases posed photos

Rishi Sunak goes on "business trip" to California for Xmas, forced early return

Stonehenge tunnel plan ruled unlawful

Grant Shapps acted "irrationally and unlawfully" in approving Stonehenge tunnel

Santander accidentally pays £130m to 75,000 customers

Stop the Steal campaign to keep Trump president

Clive Sinclair, entrepreneur (d)

Alex Scott accused by Digby Jones of ruining Olympics by dropping 'g's

Taylor Swift re-records albums over ownership row

Jussie Smollett, actor found guilty of fabricating racist, homophobic assault

Sabine Schmitz, racing driver, "Queen of the Nurburgring" (d)

Stonewall diversity scheme dropped by organisations over impartiality concerns

Squirrel gets stuck in bird feeder after eating all the nuts, Hartlepool

Substantial meal rule to drink in pubs scrapped

Sea shanties craze

Skateboarding at the Olympics

Social care crisis

Squirrel on 48 hour rampage, 18 hurt, Buckley, Wales

Second jobs, MPs scandal

Smart Motorways criticised

"Scum", Angela Raynor's summation of Tories, apologises

Steven Sondheim, composer (d)

Al Schmitt, record producer (d)

Sarah Storey, GB's most successful Paralympian

Dean Stockwell, actor (d)

Jon Snow retires from C4 News

Statue of Liberty replica loaned by France to US

Sex Pistols, John Lydon loses court case re. veto over biopic

George Segal, actor (d)

Una Stubbs, actor (d)

Marcel Stellman, record producer (d)

Ian St John, footballer (d)

Kathleen Stock, professor resigns Sussex Uni role re. gender identity views row

SAGE, government scientific advisors

Strictly Come Dancing, top 5 most watched TV show

"Sweet Caroline", unofficial England fan song, Euro 2020

Sky One closes

Spider-Man: No Way Home, world's top grossing film of the year

Strictly Come Dancing, first same sex couple

Peter Stefanovic, lawyer's Johnson lies video tweet on 43.2m views

Scratch card winners £4m denied after fraud discovered

Wilbur Smith, novelist (d)

"Stay safe", Covid advice

"Sunlit uplands" still not in view

Walter Smith, footballer (d)

Leon Spinks, boxer (d)

Sylvian Sylvain, musician (d)

Steel tariffs, US removes for EU, not UK

Space junk caused by Russia destroying satellite

Salisbury rail crash

Tom Stoltman wins World's Strongest Man competition,

Second-hand car values soar due to microchip shortage

Desmond Swayne, Tory MP criticises Afghans feeling Taliban

Sirhan Sirhan, Robert F Kennedy killer granted parole

Starlink, Elon Musk's satellites accused of hogging space

Kasper Schmeichel, goalie attacked with laser, Denmark v England, Euro 2020

"Sea snot" clogs Turkey's coasts

Shelley's eagle-owl seen in Ghana, first wild sighting since 1870s

"Spy-in-the-sky camera" to detect drivers who use a mobile phone trialed

Harry Styles' try-hard wardrobe

Seal called Freddie Mercury attacked by dog, Barnes (d)

T

Twitter bans Trump

Captain Tom Moore, man who raised £33m for NHS charities (d)

Top Shop, Oxford Circus closes

Desmond Tutu, Archbishop, South Africa (d)

Test and Trace system, £37bn and still doesn't work

Test and Trace chief Dido Harding considers applying to run NHS

Test and Trace chief Dido Harding finally steps down from NHS roles

Liz Truss says Norway, Iceland & Lichtenstein trade deal good for GB fisheries

Liz Truss' Norway, Iceland & Lichtenstein trade deal excludes fish

Liz Truss' Australia trade deal to benefit each household by £1 per year

Liz Truss' embarrassing 2014 Chatham House speech resurfaces, goes viral

Liz Truss announces pint-sized Champagne bottles as Brexit bonus

Liz Truss' Champagne pints unviable, as France decides on Champagne bottling

Liz Truss, Tory Party members' favourite to replace Johnson

Trump's Scottish golf courses' staff shortage, Brexit

Tweet, first ever by founder Jack Dorsey sells as NFT for $2.9m

£3m, Tory donors of that amount given seat in House of Lords

3D printed school, world's first, opens in Malawi

Texas abortion ruling

Trump to Georgia election official: "I just want to find 11,780 votes"

Trans rights issues

3D printed meat, largest lab-grown steak revealed

The Tulip tourist attraction skyscraper in London plan rejected

"Tampon tax" abolished

Alan Turing features on new £50 note

Truth Social, Trump's attempt to get megaphone back after Twitter ban

Trump banned from Twitter

Thomas Tuchel, new Chelsea manager wins Champions League

Tan Hill Inn, over 50 guests and an Oasis tribute band snowed in, 3 nights

Texas senator Cruz holidays in Cancun during deadly Texas winter storm

Taliban retake Afghanistan

TikTok becomes most visited website of the year

Tesla owner facing $22,000 battery replacement bill blows up car, Finland

Greta Thunberg on world leaders: "Blah, blah, blah"

Tiananmen Square memorial removed by Chinese govt. from Hong Kong Uni

Trump Jnr sent texts urging father to stop Capital riots

Three word slogans, government campaigns

Traffic light system of travel restrictions

Table service only in pubs

Trawler Cornelis Gert Jan siezed by French in Brexit fishing row

Tattoos, China bans national team footballers from having them

Turkmenistan claims zero Covid cases

Thwaites glacier, Antarctic, dubbed "doomsday glacier"

Ron Tutt, drummer (d)

Transmission rate of virus

Turkey shortage predicted at Xmas due to lack of butchers

Turkey shortage averted thanks to temporary visas for Polish workers

Thai couple marries 4 times in 37 days to maximise paid leave

Travel industry doldrums

Tomato puree and olive oil spill resembles horror scene on A14, Cambridgeshire

Trade deals post Brexit don't amount to much

Trump, second impeachment, Republicans vote not guilty

Great Thunberg not invited to Cop26

Timpson offers to pay for HRT prescriptions for staff

Dennis Thomas, musician (d)

Deezer Thompson, Deezer D, actor (d)

Brian Travers, musician (d)

B.J. Thomas, singer (d)

James Michael Taylor, actor (d)

Turing Scheme, restricted replacement for Erasmus Scheme for students

Tea consumption doubles during lockdown

Tom Tugendhat, Tory MP, emotional speech re. Afghanistan in Commons

Tropical sea turtle, world's rarest found near Rhyl after Storm Arwen

U

Universal Credit uplift cut

Ukraine border, Russian military build up

Underwear, women's thong used by man as mask on flight, kicked off

Unvaccinated, Biden says it is a pandemic of the unvaccinated

UFO files released by Pentagon

Oleksandr Usyk, heavyweight champion of the world beating Anthony Joshua

U-turns, government indecision

Universities teach remotely

Uber loses court case on UK drivers' basic rights

Unesco strips Liverpool's waterfront of world heritage status

Uyghur people persecuted in China

ULEZ boundary expanded, London

Umbrella, Johnson's "struggle" at police memorial

Utopia Planitia, landing place of China's Mars rover

United Russia, Putin's party wins election marred by fraud claims

"Unprecedented", government excuse over Covid failures

U-Roy, singer (d)

Utopia 56, humanitarian organisation sues France/UK over Channel deaths

Unboosted make up 90% of those in ICU beds by year's end

V

Virologists

Viral vector vaccines

Vaccines

Vaccination stations

"Via Getty" Twitter users mistake photo company label for name of Capitol rioter

Jean-Marc Vallee, film maker (d)

Vaccination squads, door-to-door proposal

Venezuelan migrants, nearly 2m allowed sanctuary in Columbia

Patrick Valance, physician

Vigil, top 5 most watched TV show

Virgin Galactic, commercial space flight

Max Verstappen wins F1 title

Vanilla Ice chosen by BBC to narrate podcast doc on Shergar

Ventilation, important defence against Covid

Vinyl record sales highest in 30 years

Jonathan Van-Tam, epidemiologist

VAR, football's video referee

Visas, temporary, to tempt EU workers back to help us who wanted them out

Vaccine Adverse Event Reporting System, US vaccine side-effects collator

Vaccine passports

Variants of concern

Hilton Valentine, musician (d)

Volcanos erupt: US, Spain, Papua New Guinea, Indonesia, Nicaragua

Vaccine, first for malaria endorsed by WHO

Vaccine hesitancy

Virgin Media owner merges with O2 owner

"Vacuum of integrity" Dominic Grieve on Boris Johnson

W

Claudia Webbe, MP convicted of harassment

West Virginia gives away free guns as vaccine incentive

Weetabix and beans tweet by Weetabix

Gavin Williamson out as Education Secretary

War on drugs, UK plugs away hopelessly while Europe/USA reforms

Jackie Weaver goes viral on Handforth Council Zoom meeting

"Where have you been" reporter to Johnson after 10 day absence

Charlie Watts, musician (d)

Wind, wrong kind, blamed for power cuts in North East

Walkers crisp shortage due to IT glitch

Wally the walrus tours Ireland & Britain's seas

Weatherspoons, Brexiter says pubs' beer and staff shortages "not caused by Brexit"

Wine and cheese parties at Downing Street

Murray Walker, F1 commentator (d)

"Woke", accusation levelled at anything not sufficiently right-wing

WFH, working from home

Wrexham FC bought by Ryan Reynolds and Rob McElhenney

Wrexham FC, fifth tier club catches ticket touts

Kanye West sneakers sample sells for $1.8m at auction

Kanye West Kim Kardashian announce divorce plans

West Side Story re-made by Steven Spielberg

Wallpaper, gold, No 10 refurb

"World beating" constant hollow boast of government

Chris Wallace leaves Fox News, joins rival CNN

Michael K Williams, actor (d)

WASPI, campaigners for womens' pension equality

Walkers mince pie flavoured crisps recalled over allergen mislabelling

Walkers crisp factory fire

Tiger Woods' car crash

Frank Williams, F1 team founder (d)

Winchcombe meteorite, first carbonaceous chondrite meteorite in UK

Betty White, actor (d)

Bunny Wailer, musician (d)

Whipsnade Zoo, escaped bears shot dead

Weatherspoons run out of brands of beer

Weatherspoons' pre-tax loss of £154.7m

Weatherspoons' difficulty in attracting staff

Weatherspoons' Brexiter boss claims difficulties not Brexit related

Wildfires, Australia, USA, Siberia, Europe, Asia, Africa

Wellerman sea shanty tops charts

Harvey Weinstein faces second rape trial

Roger Waters says he turned down "huge" Facebook offer to use song for ad

White supremacists, domestic terrorism threat USA

Mary Wilson, singer (d)

Chris Whitty, Covid updates

Wales rescues England with flow tests supply

Frank Worthington, footballer, scorer of "that" goal Bolton v Ipswich 1979 (d)

Windrush scandal, court rules human rights breached by Home Ofice

Martin Wood, engineer (d)

Wrong issues, Boris Johnson blames press focus for N Shropshire defeat

Wembley Stadium security lapse, Euro 2020

X

X-Factor cancelled

Xavi appointed Barcelona manager

Xi, WHO skips Greek letter for Covid variant, name of Chinese leader

X, gender-neutral "X" passport issued, first by the US

Xi Jinping

Xi'an, city of 13m in lockdown over Covid case rise

XR, Extinction Rebellion

Y

Malala Yousafzai, activist, marries

"Yes sir, I can boogie", Scottish football's unofficial anthem

Yorkshire Cricket Club racism allegations

Yellow Card Scheme, collects info on vaccine side-effects

Stephen Yaxley-Lennon aka Tommy Robinson loses libel case

Yorkshire grandmother given restraining order to stop feeding "sad" horse carrots

Yacht worth $51m sinks gas tanker after collision, Bahamas

Yemen, humanitarian catastrophe during continuing war

Yamal-Europe gas pipeline flow reversed to go east from Germany to Poland

"You" misunderstanding, Laura Ingraham's Fox News routine

"Baby Yingliang," Dinosaur embryo found in egg fossil, China

Z

Zoom meetings

Zendaya, actor dates Spider-Man co-star Tom Holland

Eric Zemmour, far-right French presidential candidate

Chloe Zhao, first woman of colour to win best director Oscar

Zoe Covid Study app identifies hotspots

Nadhim Zahawi replaces Gavin Williamson, Educ Sec

Nadhim Zahawi calls for ex-teachers to return to classrooms

Zitti E Buoni, Eurovision winning song

Zero waste, eco goal

Zombie knives, attacks

Mark Zuckerberg adds to controversial 1,500 acre Hawaii estate

Zoonotic diseases

Dana Zzyym, first person issued gender "X" passport , USA

Zoom goat, animal for hire for online meetings makes farmer £50,000

Zebra crossings, coloured, art project halted due to sight-impaired concerns

Nazanin Zaghari-Ratcliffe still detained, Iran

Printed in Great Britain
by Amazon